How to Podcast

The Equipment, Strategy & Podcasting Skills You Need to Reach Your Audience

By Colin Gray

How to Podcast

Equipment, Strategy & Skills

Copyright © Colin Gray 2013

All rights reserved. No part of this book may be reproduced or utilized in any form, electronic or mechanical, without permission in writing from the publisher.

Published by:

Wild Trails Media Publishing, Dundee
www.wildtrails.co.uk/publishing/
publishing@wildtrails.co.uk

In association with:

The Podcast Host, Dundee
www.thepodcasthost.com
info@thepodcasthost.com

To K and LB

Table of Contents

Introduction 7

What is a Podcast? 9

    What Kind of Media can Make up a Podcast? 10

    What Form does a Podcast Normally Take? 10

    What's the Difference Between an Audio File and a Podcast Episode? 12

Using Podcasts as a Listener 15

    What do I need to listen to a podcast? 15

    Listening to Podcasts on your Computer . 16

    Listening to Podcasts on the Move 17

    Automating your Podcast Listening 18

    How do I subscribe to a podcast? 19

    What If I don't have an iPod? 22

    Mobile Podcasting Apps 23

    Manually Subscribing to a Podcast 25

What Equipment Do I Need to Create a Podcast? 27

Digital Recording Devices for Podcasting .28

Mobile Phone Podcast Recording 33

Microphones 35

Podcasting Software..................................40

Recording Your Podcast 43

To Script or not to Script? 43

Your Environment 47

Editing Your Podcast 50

Music and Sound Effects 51

Editing in Audacity....................................54

Import an audio file..................................54

Playing Back Your Imported Audio...........55

Selecting, Cutting and Pasting..................56

Publishing My Podcast 76

Podcast Hosting..76

Creating a Podcast Episode Page 78

Uploading Your Audio File........................79

Getting Your Podcast Listed 83

Other Podcast Listing Services 88

Niche Directories 90
Conclusion 92
That's all folks! 92
Bonus Chapter 93
What's the Best Podcasting Microphone?
.... 93
Do I Need a Condenser Microphone for Podcasting? 94
High Quality Podcasting Microphones 96
Conclusion 100
Image Credits 102

Introduction

Hi and Welcome to 'How to Podcast'

This guide aims to get you started on the road to becoming a podcasting expert.

My name is Colin Gray and I've taught podcasting in various forms for a good few years now, most recently at University level in the UK. I have also created quite a few podcasts over the years, mostly around education, sports and business, so I'll be using all that experience to help you get started on your own podcasting journey.

I also run a website called The Podcast Host, where I offer advice and consultancy on Podcasting, as well as a number of podcasting services. Through the years I've come across just about every Podcasting question there is, and I've distilled every one of them into this simple guide to podcasting.

In this guide I'll take you from a complete

beginners level, right up to publishing your first ever podcast episode. If I've achieved my aim, by the end of this guide you'll be a confident podcaster and happy to go forth to create your own podcasting series.

Whatever your context is, I'm sure podcasts will be a great medium for getting the word out. And, on top of it all, it's great fun.

So, why wait – let's get started!

Colin - The Podcast Host

What is a Podcast?

A podcast is really just a series of audio or video recordings.

For example, BBC Radio 1 have a Podcast called 'The Best of Chris Moyles'. This podcast is a series of audio recordings from Chris Moyles' radio show, broadcasting the highlights of the show every few days.

A podcast episode is one audio or video file from that series, much the same as TV programmes have episodes which are one part of the whole series. The word 'podcast' refers to a series of audio or video files, while a 'podcast episode' is one audio file from that series.

What Kind of Media can Make up a Podcast?

As you've picked up by now, podcasts can be either audio or video. Most commonly they're in an audio format, simply because that's the easiest way to record them, and it makes them easy to use as you can listen to them on the go on your MP3 player. Some people record a series of videos though, more like a TV series, and release it as a podcast.

What Form does a Podcast Normally Take?

Podcasts, when you listen to them, are mostly very similar to radio shows. Each podcast will have a particular theme:

> e.g. mountain biking or knitting

and each podcast episode will talk about a particular subject in that theme:

> e.g. how to knit a scarf or how to jump your bike.

You'll normally have either one presenter, or a few, talking about that subject, and sometimes you'll hear interviews with guests.

Many podcasts are really simple – just a few friends chatting about a subject – and they're great and really easy to make. Some of the more professional podcasts are produced like radio and TV shows though. They can include theme music at the start, background music during the podcasts and little sound effects between interviews or sections. They sound great, but they take a lot longer to produce.

What's the Difference Between an Audio File and a Podcast Episode?

One of the things people find most confusing about podcasts is how they differ from normal audio or video files. Well, this is both pretty simple and a bit complicated at the same time.

The simple answer is that a podcast episode is just an audio file which you can subscribe to. This is done through a technology called RSS (the complicated bit…) but, the good thing is, you don't need to worry too much about the feed itself, it's handled for you if you use a podcast hosting website.

I'll explain a bit more about RSS feeds in the

'Using a Podcasts as a Listener' section.

It basically means that you have a list of podcasts that you have subscribed to, and new episodes of those podcasts automatically appear on your computer when they're released. With normal audio files you would have to search them out on the web and download them yourself, but RSS feeds allow all of that to be done for you.

The main thing to remember is, an audio file on its own is just an audio file.

But, an audio file which is uploaded to a website and included in an RSS feed so that people can subscribe to it – that's a podcast!

Using Podcasts as a Listener

What do I need to listen to a podcast?

There are a few different ways that you can listen to a podcast, and some of them depend on how the podcast makers are publishing their podcast.

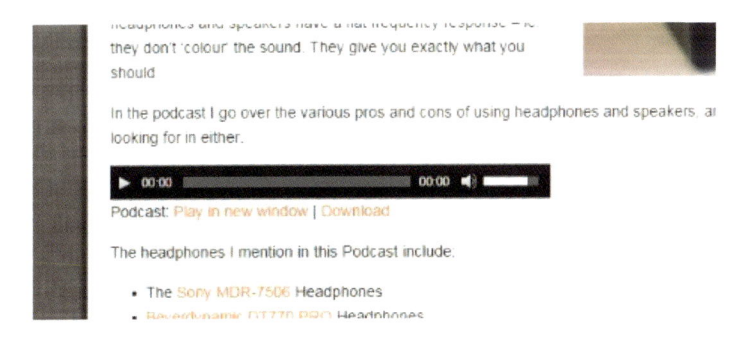

The image above shows a typical podcast player, as seen on a podcasting website.

Some don't require any more equipment than a PC or a Mac, and some require a bit of extra equipment and software.

Let's look at the options.

Listening to Podcasts on your Computer

The simplest way to listen to a podcast is just to navigate your way to the website on which it's hosted, find the episode you want to listen to, and hit the play button. That's it!

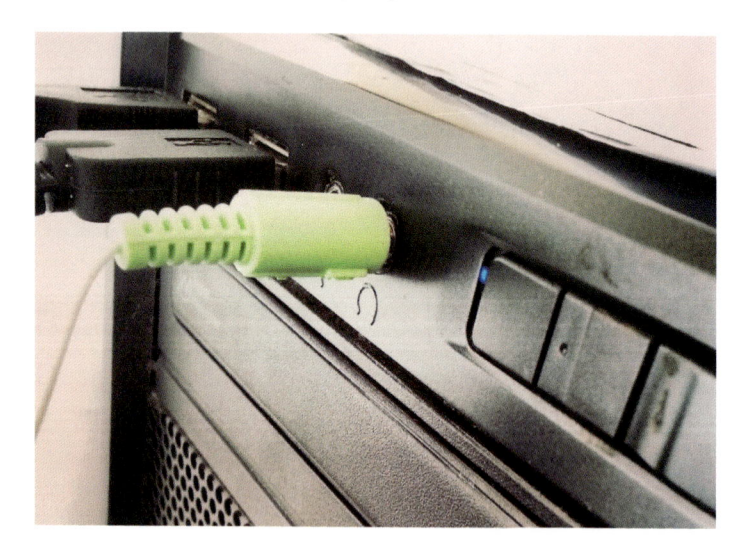

All you need for this method is a PC or a Mac and an internet connection.

Most podcast websites will allow you to play the podcast episodes directly on the web page. But, obviously that means you're tied down to your PC which isn't very flexible.

Listening to Podcasts on the Move

Often the best way to listen to a podcast is to load it onto an MP3 player of some sort so that you can play it while you're out and about. This means downloading the podcast from the website somehow.

We've talked about subscription, but I'll get to that in a bit, because the simplest way is to just to download the podcast directly from the webpage mentioned above.

Normally the page that allows you to play the

podcast will also allow you to download it. So, you can download the podcast to your computer, transfer it to your player, whether it's a MP3 player, an iPod or your mobile phone, and listen to it straight away.

For this method you need a computer, an internet connection and a digital mp3 player (mobile phone, iPod, etc)

Automating your Podcast Listening

Of course, the most powerful way to listen to a podcast is to use all the powers of the RSS feed, automating the whole process. This takes a bit more setting up and requires extra software, but if you listen to a lot of podcasts, and particularly if you want to keep up with the whole series, then it's the best way in the long run.

Sometimes, of course, you won't need to go this far and it's easiest just to download one here or there, but it's worth covering.

How do I subscribe to a podcast?

To subscribe to a Podcast you need special software called a podcatcher. Examples of these are iTunes or Juice, but there are a range of options out there.

Many music players have added podcatching capabilities to their range of options, Winamp being a good example. Most of these options are free so you don't have to pay a penny to get podcasting.

Let's take iTunes as an example of a pod catcher. It's one of the most powerful examples thanks to its great podcast directory, included in the iTunes store. Plus, it's almost certainly the most widely used.

To subscribe you simply go to the iTunes store, and type the subject you're searching for into the search box.

For example, I'm going to search for a Web Design podcast to keep up to date with my work.

The process is:

1. I navigate to the Podcast section of the iTunes store, then type 'web design' into the search box.
2. Once I've done this iTunes will bring up all podcasts that include that phrase in the title or description.
3. I see one called The Boagworld Show, and click on that title or icon.

4. ITunes shows me the list of episodes in that Podcast series and I can browse through.
5. If I like what I see, I press the Subscribe button, and that podcast is added to my subscribe list.
6. I go back to the search results and do the same with 'Think Vitamin' and 'The Sitepoint Podcast'.
7. Then, upon clicking the Podcast section in the iTunes menu I see these three podcasts in my subscribe list.

Now, whenever I have iTunes running, it'll regularly check for new episodes of each of these podcasts. When I plug in my iPod, iTunes will delete old episodes that I have already listened to and send new episodes to my iPod, all ready for listening to when I'm next out. I never need to check for new episodes again – the newest episodes will always be available to me on my player.

For this method you need a computer, an internet connection, a digital mp3 player

and a pod catcher application

What If I don't have an iPod?

If you're not using an apple device you wont be able to use iTunes, but have no fear, there are plenty of good options out there. For example, Samsung produces it's own iTunes equivalent called Kies.

Download and install Kies, and straight away you're ready to subscribe to Podcasts, just as in iTunes, and have the automatically sync with your phone.

It's outside the scope of this book to list every Podcast management app for every device, but it's definitely worth a look on the manufacturer's site in the first instance. And if that doesn't work, try googling "podcast app X" where X is the name of your device.

And if that fails, well have a look at the next section – there's a better alternative!

Mobile Podcasting Apps

The alternative to computer based software is to use a mobile Podcasting app. This means that you have an application on your phone or device that manages all your podcast subscriptions. So you never need to plug your device into the computer again. Much easier!

Apple have their own Podcasting app which offers a nice alternative to iTunes. It still takes advantage of the iTunes store catalogue though, so it has an excellent directory, and is one of the best Podcasting apps out there.

If you have an Android device, though, don't worry. There are some excellent Podcasting tools on the Android platform.

BeyondPod is my favourite Podcasting app and the one I use to manage my own podcasts. It actually has a lot more flexibility than the Apple app, and is far more powerful. All if lacks is a really comprehensive directory, just relying on a slightly less powerful search. You can get around that, though. just by searching for your Podcasts on the web, or even using the iTunes store to search, and then copying over the feed URL.

Another alternative is DoggCatcher, and there are a few more out there too. Stitcher gets a special mention as a great Podcast distributer, and it has its own mobile app. The directory is more limited than most, but it hosts some great Podcasts.

Manually Subscribing to a Podcast

So it is possible to automatically subscribe to a Podcast, whether it's through the iTunes store, the BeyondPod search, or otherwise. Sometimes, though, whatever platform you're using, you wont be able to find the podcast you're looking for. In this case you need to manually add a podcast to the player.

This is accomplished by copying the web address (or URL) of the podcast RSS feed and pasting it into the pod catcher. All pod catchers will have a pretty prominent option to 'Add a Podcast.' Upon selecting that it will ask for the RSS feed address.

You can normally find a podcast's RSS feed address by looking at the website and following links to 'Subscribe'. It's often very well advertised.

Other times you should look for the RSS icon, which is shown here. After clicking that icon you are normally taken to the RSS feed page. You can just copy the address of that page from the address bar in the browser and put it into your pod catcher.

What Equipment Do I Need to Create a Podcast?

You'll be pleased to find out that creating your own podcast is amazingly easy, and requires very little equipment. Even better, the equipment you do require is often already available to you.

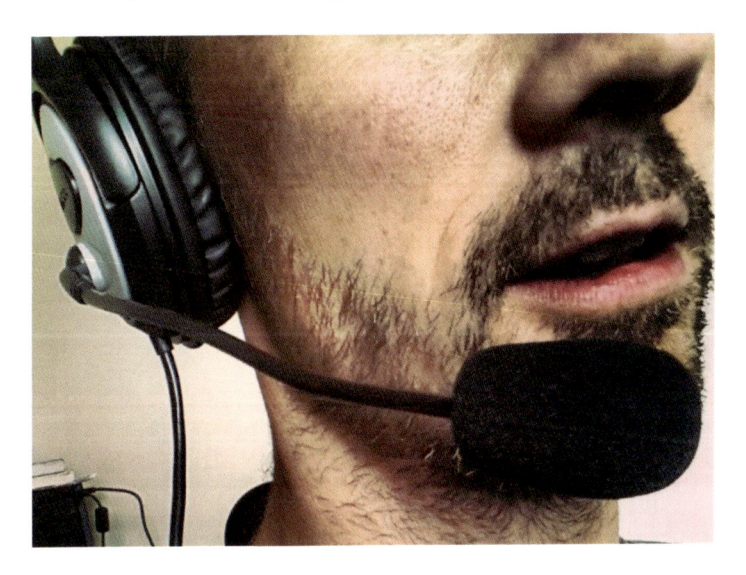

In this section I'll go through exactly what you need to create your own podcast and where you could go about finding it.

Digital Recording Devices for Podcasting

The most basic thing you need for any podcast is a recording device. Naturally, to create an audio file, you need to be able to record your voice!

Recording devices take many forms, from really simple Dictaphones to full-quality professional audio recorders.

Plus, your computer can act as a recording device – it's easily possible to record a regular podcast using no more than a laptop and its inbuilt microphone.

For good results, it's normally desirable to have at least a simple mobile recording device. Without a recorder that you can carry around, you'll be stuck to your computer desk for all your podcast creation and, especially with a group, that's often not ideal.

It's worth spending more than the minimum on a recording device as the quality is very dependent on price. Moving above the £50+ mark generally takes you into the range of good quality recorders, and you can spend infinitely more than that it you try.

Professional journalist level kit of this sort sells for £300 or £400 and comes with all sorts of features. I'll mention one of this sort at the end of the section, but you shouldn't feel any pressure to jump in at that level.

To get started, just buy what you can afford, or use the equipment you already have available. Better to get started with basic kit than not at all!

For my lower cost device, I use a Sony IC Recorder (ICD-UX71) – shown here.

This costs around £60 to £70 and gives a great quality sound for the price. It has a USB port on the bottom so you can plug it straight into your computer, and it has an external microphone socket so you can always plug a better quality mic in at a later date if you decide you need the sound quality improved.

For a higher end device, better quality sound and more recording options, look at the Roland R-05.

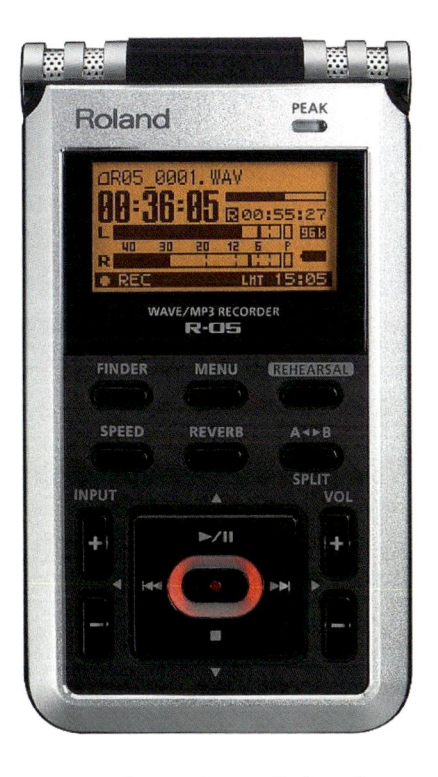

It's about twice the price of the Sony, and I find it a great little recorder. The sound quality is definitely better than the Sony, although only noticeable when you compare them side by side and it just offers a few more options when you're doing your recordings.

The Roland comes in around £140 on Amazon and would do perfectly for anyone, even approaching professional journalist level.

For the real top-level though, in my opinion, you're looking at the Zoom H4n recorder, shown above. It has an excellent quality set of internal mics, various options for external mics and tons of tools packed within the make your out-of-the-office recording much easier.

The H4n allows you to record using professional level microphones too, offering two XLR connections. You don't need to worry too much about what that means right now, but suffice to say that if bought this recorder, you wont need to upgrade it once you move up to professional levels of recording and other equipment.

This is the journalist level device I mentioned earlier and could be used to prepare a feature for the BBC, if you ever get the chance!

Mobile Phone Podcast Recording

If, however, you don't fancy spending any money on podcasting, you could look at the equipment you already have. Mobile phones are great recording devices, and it makes sense considering they're built purely for recording and transmitting your voice.

Pretty much any smart phone will have a voice recording capability, and devices like the iPhone or Samsung Galaxy have great recording and editing facilities.

They also let you email the file to yourself straight away so you always have a backup in case you lose the device.

Even if you don't have a smart phone, many older phones can still act as a Dictaphone. Have a browse through your phone menu and you might find an audio recording or

Dictaphone function that you never knew you had.

Microphones

One great addition to your podcasting kit list, if you have the money, is an external microphone. Even a low-cost microphone can hugely increase the ease and quality of your recordings.

All of the recorders above can take external mics and will benefit from using one. Saying that, bear in mind that you would need a very good quality mic to improve upon the H4n's internal offering.

If you're recording from a computer, you'll almost certainly need an external microphone. The microphones built into laptop PCs are normally very low quality and aren't worth using.

For computer recording, you have a huge range of options. A standard headset microphone – the type you would use with Skype - will do the job pretty well. Canyon headsets, available for around £15 on

Amazon, create a decent quality recording.

Some headset mics can be very tinny, though, so it's worth sticking with the Canyon, or finding yourself a Microsoft Livechat mic. The Livechat is another good quality headset mic for only £20 to £30.

The downside of the Livechat is that it's USB only. If you're only planning to record via the computer, that's fine – it does make it very easy to set up and doesn't rely on your audio settings.

But, if you're out and about and want to plug in an external microphone to your recorder, you'll need the Canyon's standard headphone jack.

If you're looking for the next level up, however, you could go for the Samson Go Mic as shown. This is another USB microphone, and produces excellent results for the price.

It's also really flexible in that it comes with an

in-built mic clip, so you can stick it to just about anything and make it very easy to record with.

If you'll be doing a lot of work out-of-the-office with your digital recorder, you might want to get a more traditional looking microphone.

The audio technical ATR 6250 is a reasonably low-cost mic which plugs into any recorder with a small mic jack (same as your headphone socket) and if you spend much above that you're usually guaranteed a good quality as long as it's from a good brand.

Microphones are surprisingly technical bits of kit and there are all sorts of variations and configurations, but you can get a good one for less than £50 so don't worry too much about the higher end ones when you first start out. Often it's more about your environment than the microphone when it comes to final recording quality, as we'll discuss in the recording chapter.

If you are interested in upgrading and want to get yourself a really professional quality mic, have a look at the Bonus microphones chapter later in the book.

Podcasting Software

In ideal circumstances, you can actually create a podcast without any software at all. You could make a recording and upload it to your podcasting hosting space straight away, with no editing. This depends on you being pretty accurate with your recording of course, and making no slips or mistakes!

In reality, people make mistakes and you often need to make edits to an audio file before you publish it. You may also want to add music or sound effects to a podcast, or to stitch two separate audio files together, such as your introduction and an interview you did at another time.

In this case, you need audio editing software. The good thing is, it's an easy choice.

If you don't already have an audio editing package, then Audacity is the package for you. It's powerful, it does everything you need, and, best of all, it's free!

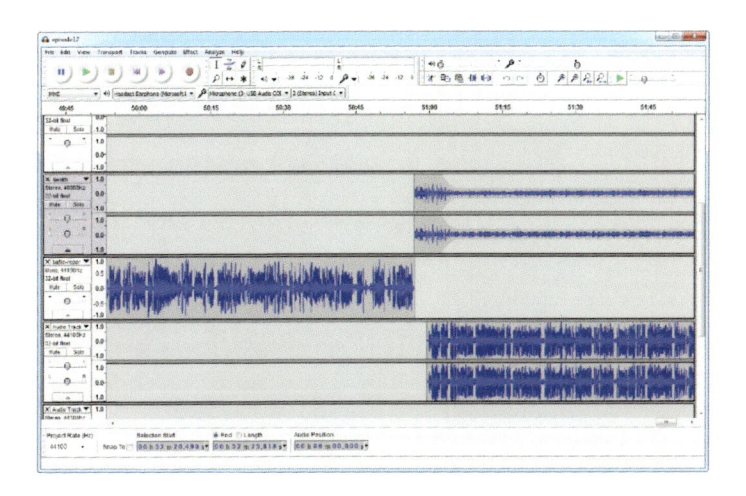

You can download a copy of audacity at: http://audacity.sourceforge.net/

Audacity works on both Mac and PC, so you don't need to worry about the platform. That's why it's the software that I teach, and the one I cover in this book. It's open, it's flexible and it's available to anyone, which counts for a lot.

If you're on a Mac, however, Garageband is a very popular alternative. It's a really easy to use, powerful bit of software, and best of all, it's free!

On the PC, the next up the list from Audacity, for me, would be Adobe Audition. It's not a cheap bit of software, but it's very good. Many people claim Audacity is just as powerful, however, or even more so, so it can be hard to justify the cost.

If you use other Adobe software you might have Audition packaged in though, so in that case it's worth a try.

Whatever you choose, that's all we need to get started – on to recording!

Recording Your Podcast

It's time to grab a glass of water, warm up that voice and get recording! In this section we'll look at how to go about recording your podcast, including scripting and how to set up your recording space.

To Script or not to Script?

This is the question asked by every would-be podcaster, and one of the most debated areas of podcasting prep. Should you write a full script?

Fortunately, the answer is easy, if not very helpful – it depends on what you're comfortable with!

I know a number of podcasters that hardly write anything down. They know their subject back to front and they just go into the recording with a broad outline of what they'll talk about. They might have 4 or 5 bullet points, and they come across great on air – smooth and friendly.

The spontaneous and unplanned nature of this approach makes the podcast sound really personal and engaging, and, if done well, it can sound great. Also, it takes very little prep. You can create a podcast very quickly using this method.

The downside of this approach is that, without a script, expert or not, you'll often stumble over your words, run out of things to say, or simply forget to cover everything you planned to. It can be quite hard to do a 20 minute podcast with just a very broad outline.

Alternatively, I also know podcasters that write everything down, word for word, even having done it for years. They'll have a full script and read it out slowly and surely, sounding very articulate and expert. Everything will be perfect, no points missed, and the podcast will go exactly as you plan.

The downside of this is that it takes a long time to prepare. You're carrying out two tasks – writing an essay on your subject, and then speaking it out. Added to that, when reading a script, you can often sound pretty un-spontaneous, flat and even robotic. It can be less engaging than off-the-cuff speech and definitely less friendly.

In reality, a blend is often best.

You can write a script with is bullet pointed, but with a fair bit of detail. Don't write it down word for word, but have a prompt for each paragraph so that you know where you're going. This way you won't miss anything, but you'll hopefully avoid the monotone reading-voice problem.

Your Environment

Even though we've talked about the quality offered by recording equipment, microphones and software, one of the biggest factors in how your recording will sound is your environment.

Thinking about where you do your recordings is really important for good quality sound.

Here are a few things to think about when choosing where to do your recording:

1. Background noise is far more obvious on a recording. Watch out for:

- Corridors with people walking by often
- Windows close by with a busy road outside
- Computers or other equipment running in the background
- Large lights making a buzzing sound

2. Echoes can really reduce the quality of your recording:

- Try to record in a large room, not facing the wall
- Or try to record in a room with soft walls – wood or wallpaper

Here are a few things to think about when doing your recording:

The presenters themselves are normally the biggest cause of unwanted noise:

- Rustling of paper or jangling of keys by presenters or guests

- Coughing, sniffing and heavy breathing
- Fumbling the microphone, or moving the recorder

The main thing is to be aware that any noise is very easily picked up by the microphone. You want the room you choose to be as quiet as possible, and you want the others in the room to be as careful as they can not to make unnecessary noise.

Editing Your Podcast

One you've finished your recording, it's time to turn it into an edited podcast. This is where you take out any mistakes, stick together different audio recordings and add any music or sound effects.

An Editing Proviso...

Now the main thing to remember here is that's there's no need to go overboard. Many successful podcasts do very little editing. In fact, if you're looking just to get your information out there, you might not need to do any editing at all.

Music, FX and multiple features are all well and good, but the key to podcasting success is longevity. Whatever process allows you to create decent, regular Podcasts is the one for you. And if that means no title music, and no editing, then that's fine. As long as your content is good, and the quality of audio recording is decent, then you'll do well.

But, to add a bit of a professional finish, there's nothing like a bit of music, some FX and tying together a few different audio clips, such as introductions, interviews and features.

Let's see how it's done.

Music and Sound Effects

Music can make a big difference to how professional and engaging your podcast sounds. A short 10 second musical intro can really make your podcast stand out from the crowd, and that audio can be used at different points as background music to make it sound even more professional. Sounds effects too can really enhance your podcast, offering a little buffer between one audio recording and the next - your introduction and an interview, for example.

There are a number of places to locate royalty free music on the web. Most of them require you to simply credit the creator of the music on your website or on the podcast, and then you can use the music as much as you like for free.

Have a look at these sites for some good choices:

- http://incompetech.com/m/c/royalty-free/
  A good site for royalty free music. All tunes are available for free use as long as you credit the creator.
- http://www.jamendo.com/
  This site has thousands of albums worth of music free to use for various purposes as long as you credit the creator. It's mostly under creative commons licensing.
- http://www.partnersinrhyme.com/pir/free_music_loops.shtml
  Has some good music loops and a number of sound effects.
- http://www.sounddogs.com/
  Great for simple sound effects for any video project.

Editing in Audacity

Audacity is a really simple audio editor to use, but it does take a short time to figure out the tools. The creators of Audacity have created a great set of documentation which you can access here:

http://audacity.sourceforge.net/manual-1.2/

I have put together a short set of instructions below too to get you started. This is what you'll need for your first few podcasts and covers the basic editing tasks.

Import an audio file

The first thing you need to do is import the audio files that you've recorded. This may just be one recording, for some quick editing, or you might be putting together a few different recordings into one podcast.

To bring the files into Audacity do one of the following:

1. Select *Import Audio ...* in the File menu, and choose your file(s).

2. Use the keyboard shortcut: CTRL+I

Audacity can import WAV, AIFF, AU, IRCAM, MP3 and OGG files.

Normally you'll only be working with either WAV or MP3 files as these are the most commonly created by both audio recorders, and recording software.

Playing Back Your Imported Audio

The imported audio file should now be displayed in an audio track. The track will look a little like this, depending on what you imported:

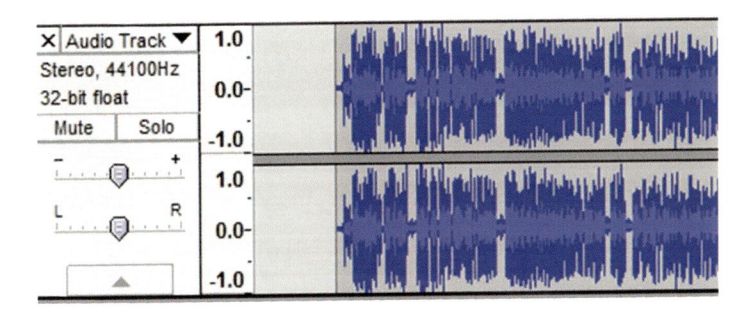

Now if you click the green Play button at the top and you should hear the file you have just imported. This lets you play through and find out what parts you need to edit.

Selecting, Cutting and Pasting

The most basic editing option that you'll want to carry out is cutting. This means taking out unwanted parts of the track. You might want to do this because you coughed during the recording, or you simply made a mistake that you want to remove.

Either way, to get rid of the offending bit of audio, you need to select it and cut it.

Making a selection

To select the part you wish to cut, copy or paste to, use the selection tool I. If it's not activated, you can choose it by clicking on the icon in the toolbar.

Now you'll click and drag the cursor over the

part you want to select, much as you would in the wordprocessor document if you want to select a sentence.

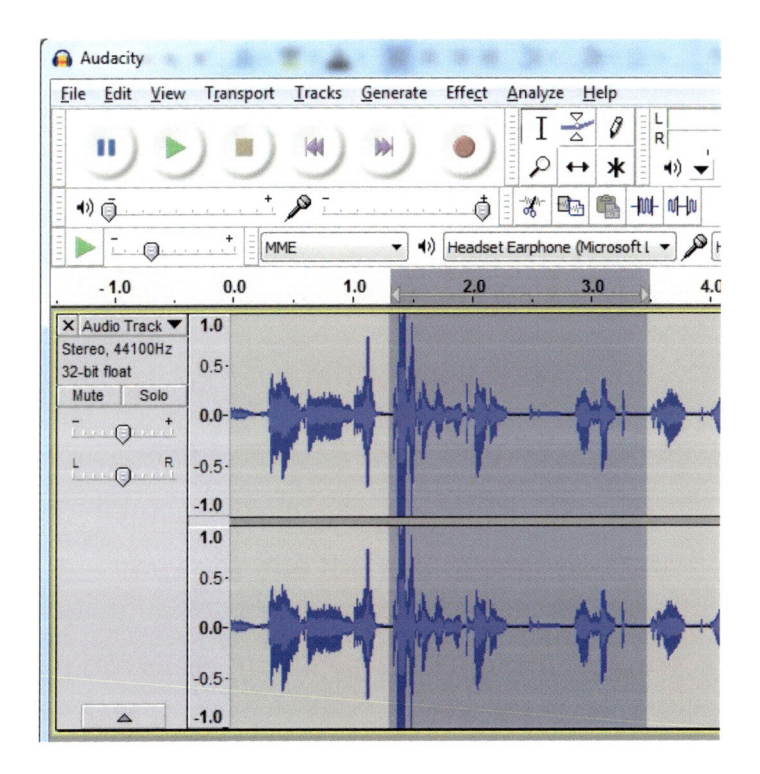

The selected area will appear darker than the surrounding area of the clip. You can select a part and keep dragging right to select a large section of the clip. This will cause Audacity to scroll right for you until you've found the end of your selection.

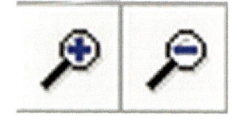

I'd advise zooming out, though, so that you can see your full selection before starting Playback.

You'll have to find a balance between zooming out to see the whole selection, and zooming in enough to find the quiet point between the words or sentence that you've recorded.

Normally the best place to cut is when there is silence, and that's represented by the wave form dropping down to nothing, as shown by the arrows in the image below.

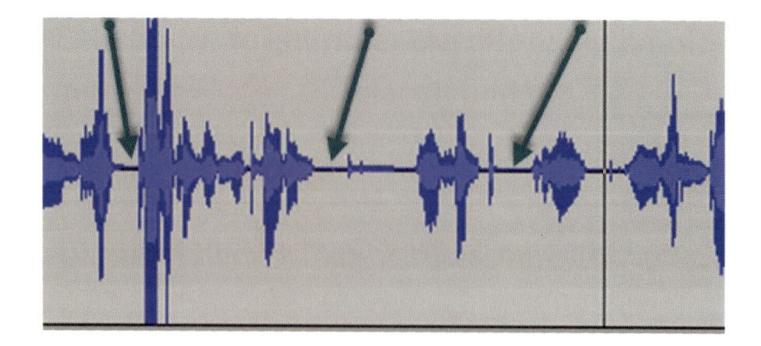

As a little trick, you can now press the space bar to listen to the audio in the selected area. This helps to make sure you've got the right part.

To **extend** or **contract** your selection, you can hold down the SHIFT button and click on the location where you want the selection boundary to move to.

If you click at a spot that is on the right hand side from the middle of the current selection, you will set the right hand boundary of your new selection, and vice versa for the left.

Cutting the Selected Area

You can cut the selected area in 3 ways:

1. selecting "**Cut**" from the **Edit > Remove Audio or Labels** menu

2. pressing **CTRL+X (cmd-x on Mac)**

3. pressing the Delete key on your keyboard

After you have cut out a selection, listen to the audio around the cut to make sure it sounds ok. If you've accidentally cut in the middle of a word, and it's very obvious, then you can always undo the action and try again. Click undo in the edit menu to do that.

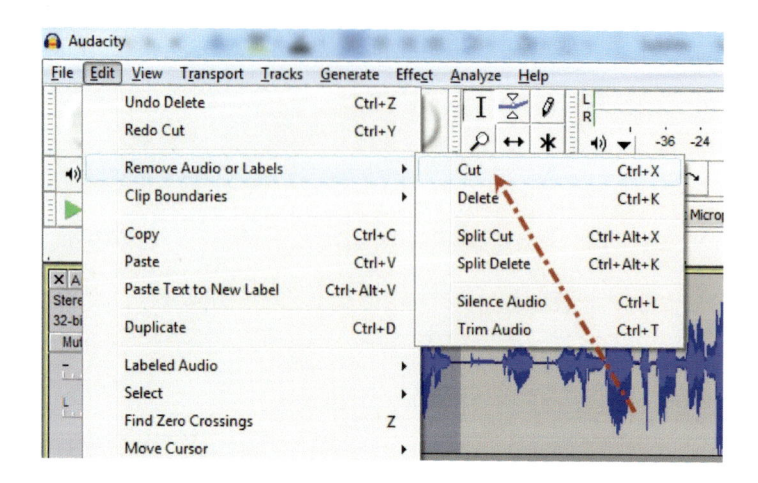

Copying the Selected Audio

Instead of cutting a part of the audio out entirely, you might want to copy it elsewhere.

Once you've made your selection, **"Copy"** will copy the selection to the clipboard.

You can then **"Paste"** that selection back into any track by clicking where you want it to be placed, and then selecting **Paste** in the Edit menu.

Mixing Background Music with a Voiceover

Audacity makes it really easy to mix two different sounds together. This is called multitrack editing, and is a level up from simple audio editing. If you get this far, then well done!

Here are the steps to follow:

1. Open your main audio file (for example, the interview you recorded last week).

2. Select Import Audio... from the File menu and open the sound you want to play alongside (for example, the background music).

3. Listen to tracks using Play button. **Audacity** will have automatically placed them alongside each other and you'll hear them playing at the same time. You can see both tracks in the play window, one on top of the other, as shown in the screenshot below.

It seems that you can see 4 tracks, but that's because both tracks are stereo, so you have two channels on each track. You can see there are only two tracks because each track has one boxed area on the right, with the track title at the top – "Audio Track" as shown below.

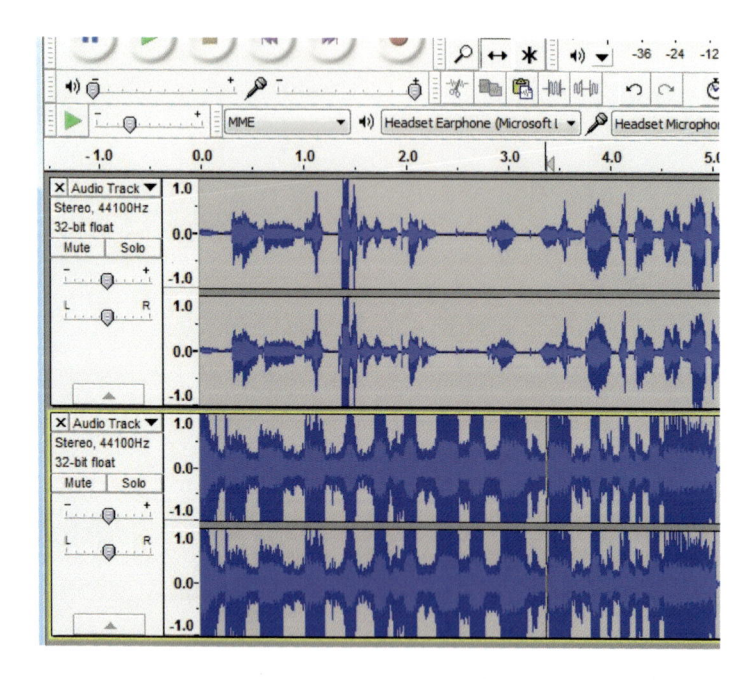

4. Choose the Time Shift tool ↔ and adjust the position of one track or the other by dragging it left or right. Move the tracks until they're synchronized as you have planned, so that the music starts and stops when you want it to.

5. Edit the music to suit the length required. You can shorten the music simply by selecting a portion of it and cutting it out. Find the point you want it to stop, select from there right up to the end, and pressing the delete key.

Working with Music Volume in Podcasts

Music has 2 main purposes in a Podcast:

1. Background music, to play constantly alongside a voice track.

2. Introduction or outro music, to mark the start and the end of your podcast.

In both cases, you'll need to edit the volume in some way.

For background music, you'll need to make it quieter, so that it doesn't drown out the voice track.

And for intro and outro music, you'll want to make it fade in and out to blend in with the voice tracks that it brackets. Let's have a look at how to do this.

Editing Background Music Volume

Background music is quite simple, you just need to reduce the volume of the entire track.

This is done using the **Gain** control, on the left hand panel of each track. You can see this slider indicated by the arrow in the image below.

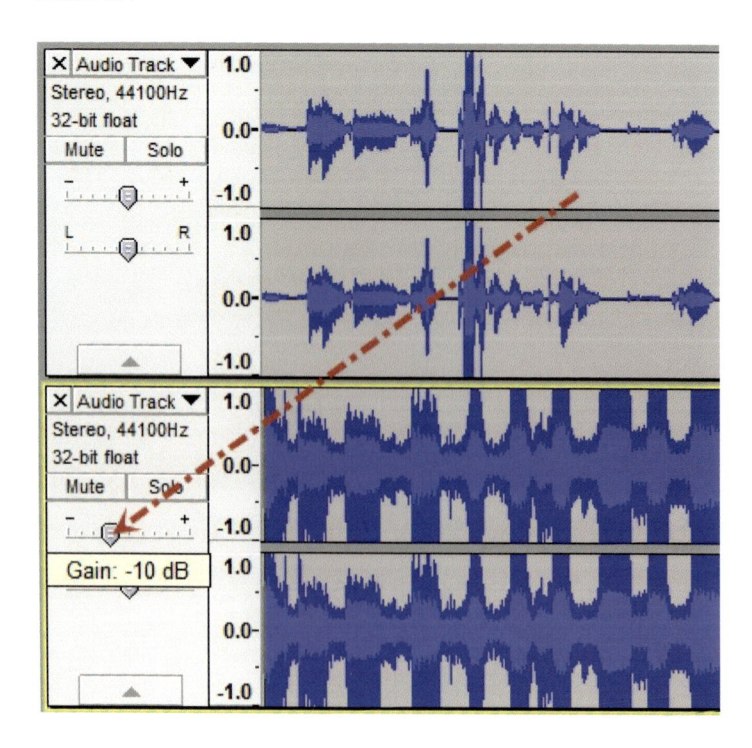

Slide that control left to reduce the volume and right to increase it.

The easiest way to find the right level is to press Play, listen to the audio and move the slider left and right until you hear a good level.

Make sure you have the background music quiet enough so that the voices are really easy to hear.

Using The Fade Tool to Control Volume

For intro and outro music, normally you want to play the music for a short time at the start, and then fade it out as you start to speak.

This can be done quite easily using the fade tool.

Firstly, decide on how long the intro music will play. 10 to 20 seconds is normally plenty. Then, select the last 5 seconds or so of the music track. This is area that will fade out. If you want a longer fade, so that it overlaps with the voice for longer, then keep a longer section of music at the start of the track, and select a longer area to Fade. Once you've selected an area to fade out, click the **Effects Menu > Fade Out** tool, as shown below.

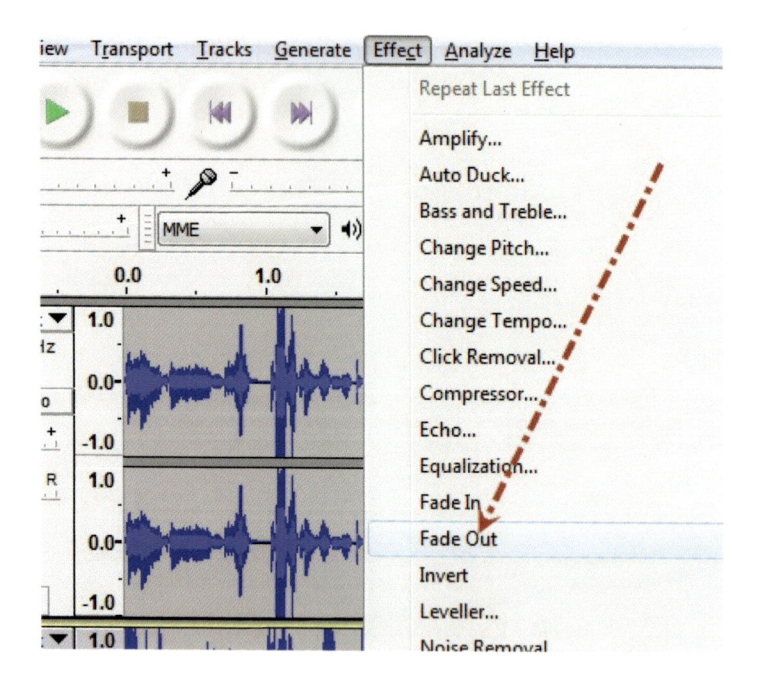

This will make the entire selected area start off at its normal volume and then gradually fade away to silence. You can see how this looks in the following image. The arrow shows the selected and fading area.

Now the only thing to do is to move the voice

track to follow the Fading section, and you're done.

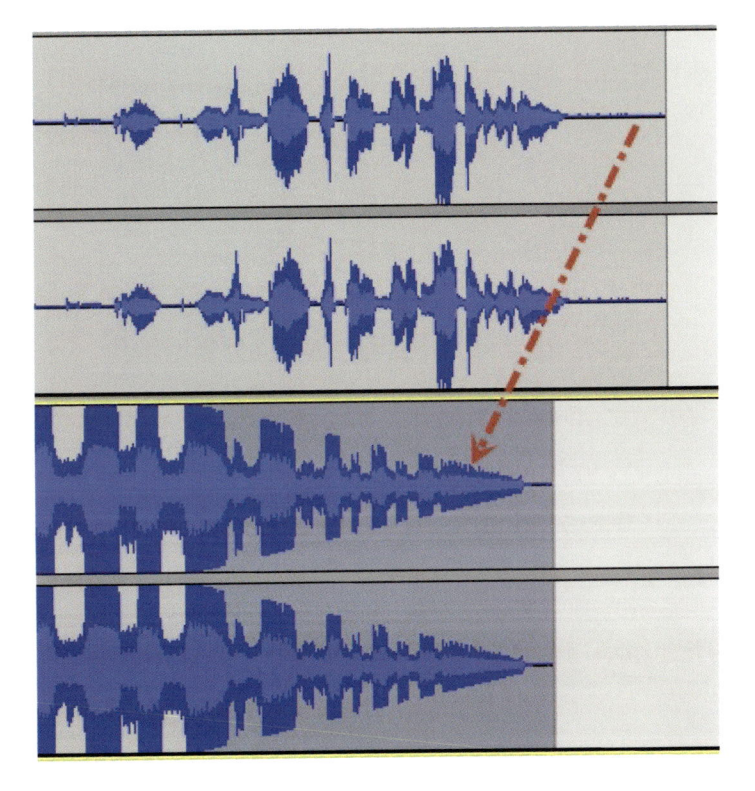

You can get the best results here by overlapping the start of the voice track with the fading area. This means the voice starts speaking as the music is fading out, and creates a nice professional sounding intro.

To do this, use the time shift tool to move the

voice track to the right, until the start of it lies just beyond the start of the music fade. You can see how this looks in the image below.

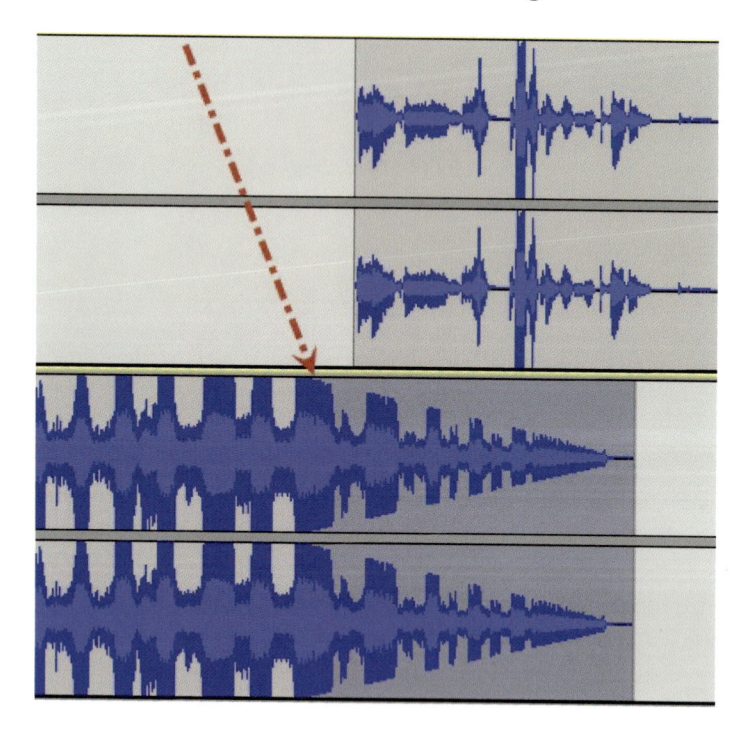

The red arrow shows where the fade begins, and so I've dragged the voice along to the right so that it starts just after the fade begins. Try this out and you'll be amazed how professional you sound already!

You can do the exact opposite for your outro music using the **Fade In** tool. This appears, too, in the **Effect** menu. Just select the start portion of your outro music, click the Fade In tool, and it'll start the track at zero volume, and gradually increase it over the time period that you selected.

Using the Envelope Tool For Intro/Outro Music Volume Control

Sometimes you'll want a bit more control over the volume of a track. An example of this might be an intro where you have 30 seconds of music, but for 10 seconds in the middle of that music, you give a short introduction to the podcast.

This is a very common introduction to professional podcasts and really makes an episode shine when you can pull it off.

Luckily it's pretty easy! You do this using the envelope tool.

First, get your music, and place it at the start of your track. Then get your short vocal introduction, and drag it to overlap the middle of the music intro, as shown.

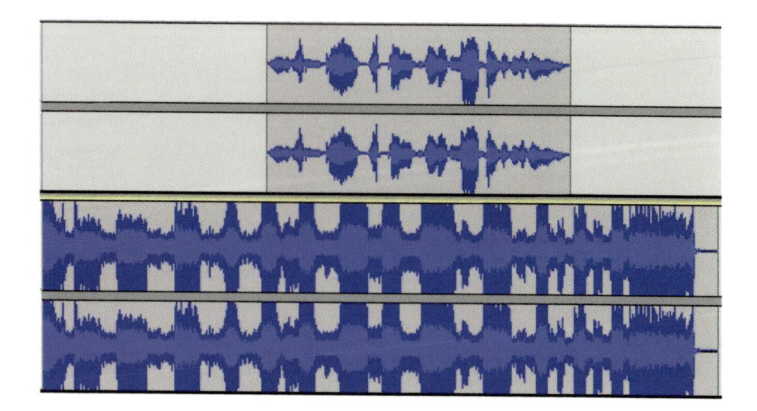

If you play the audio now, you'll barely hear the voice as the music will be too loud. What you need to do it reduce the volume of the music just for the section where the voice is speaking.

To do this, select the Envelope tool.

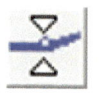

Now, you'll see the track is bounded, top and bottom, by a blue line. Click on this blue line with the envelope tool at the point which you wish the music to start fading down.

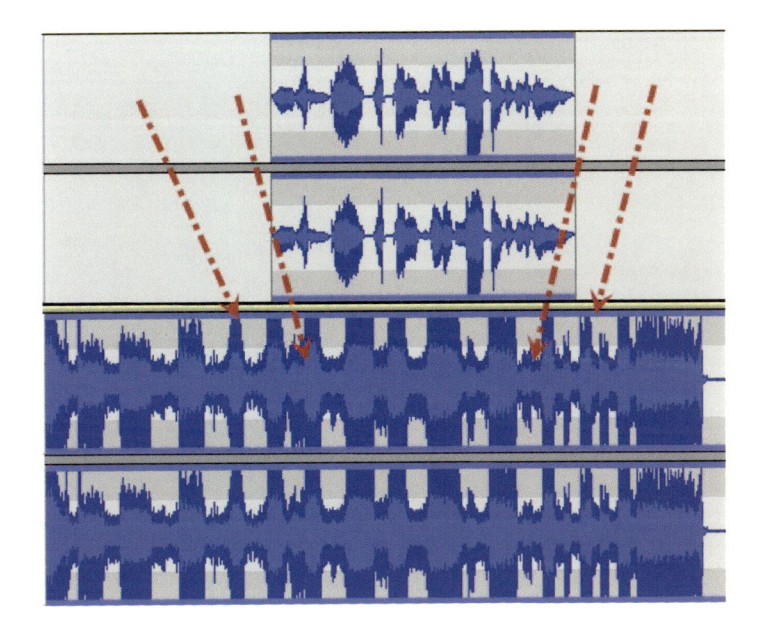

This point is shown by the left-most arrow in the image above. Next, click just after the vocals start, where you want the music to finish fading down. This is shown by the second red arrow from the left.

When you do this, you'll see small white dots appear on the blue line, as shown by the arrow below. If you click and drag these dots up and down, you can change the volume of the music at that point in the track.

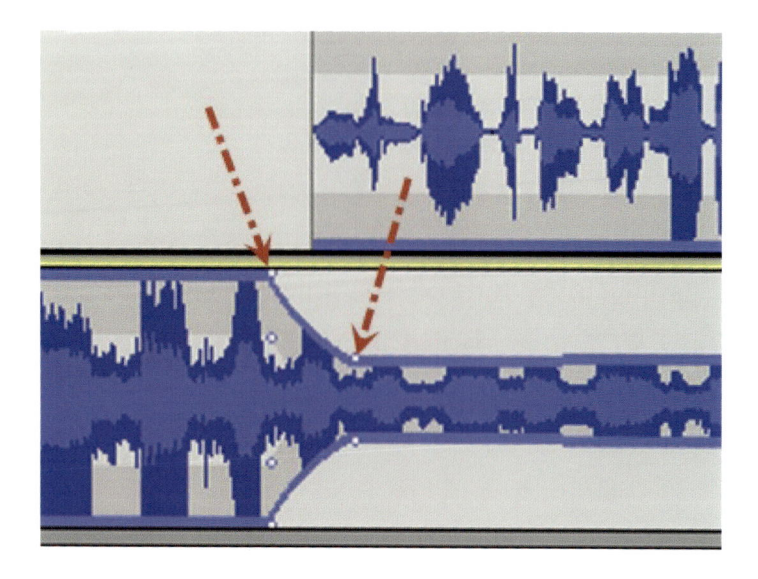

Dragging the white dots towards the centre makes the music quieter. The results are shown in the image above – this is how your intial fade-out should appear. You can see the music starts out loud, then just before the vocal starts (the topmost track) the music starts to reduce in volume. Then a little after the vocal starts, it levels out and remains playing, but quietly.

You simply do the opposite for the fade back up, once the vocals finish. Click on the blue line just before the voice stops, then again just after the voice stops. Lastly, drag the white dot right after the voice stops up to the top of track, so that volume increases.

Your track shown now look similar to the image above, and sound very professional!

This can work quite well for outro music too. Outro music works well when faded in quite early and played over your entire closing section of the podcast. This is normally where you talk about the next episode or ask for feedback and give out your contact details.

Use your envelope tool to fade up your outro music to a low volume level at the start of your closing section. Then, once you stop speaking, fade it up to full volume, play for 5 to 10 seconds and then stop the music altogether. This gives a great, professional sounding outro.

Exporting your Finished Podcast

Once you've done all of your editing, it's time to export the finished article!

To export your podcast click on **File > Export**. This will allow you to choose where to save the file.

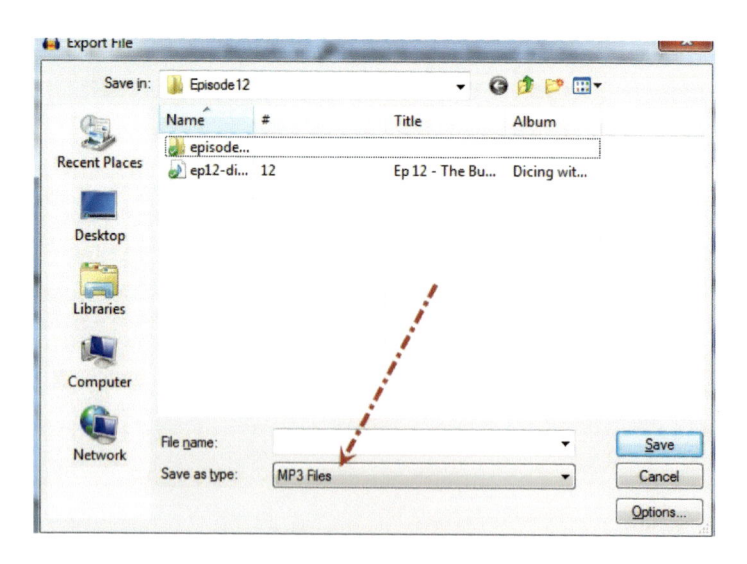

The important thing here is to make sure you choose the MP3 format, as shown above. This is the most commonly used format for podcasting, and is the one that every digital player will be able to process.

Publishing My Podcast

Once you've recorded your podcast, edited it and saved it as an MP3, it's time to publish it to a Podcast Hosting site so that your willing public can listen to your efforts.

Podcast Hosting

In order to store your podcast episodes and deliver them through an RSS feed, you need a special podcast hosting space. This allows you to upload your podcast episodes, put a little intro text alongside them and then publish them for all to hear.

Once published, the podcast hosting site will organise the RSS feed and make sure anyone can subscribe to your podcast if they so choose.

There are a few options for Podcast Hosting sites, but I'm going to talk about process you'll follow when using The Podcast Host.

The Podcast Host is an easy-to-use system and is based on the Wordpress framework. Many Podcasting sites use Wordpress as a base, so the process I cover next will be very similar to other Podcasting sites out there.

Obviously it's up to you who you go with though, and there are quite a few alternatives that you'll find easily online. Whichever you choose, you'll be asked to create an account, after which you'll have a site set up for you.

Creating a Podcast Episode Page

Once your podcasting space is set up, it's time to post a podcast to that space. Podcasting works in a similar way to blogging. You create a page, commonly called a post, which contains some text and a link to your podcast.

The text is quite important as it forms a guide to the podcast episode, and entices people in to listen to it. Here are some good things to include on a podcast episode page:

- Write an introduction to the podcast, offering a brief summary of the subject
- Include a time schedule of the show, showing when each section starts so that the listener can quickly fast forward through if they want to hear a particular section
- Include a request for feedback, either through comments or email.

On The Podcast Host, to create a new Episode Page, click **'Podcast'** on the left hand menu, and then **'Add New'**. This will produce a screen like the one below.

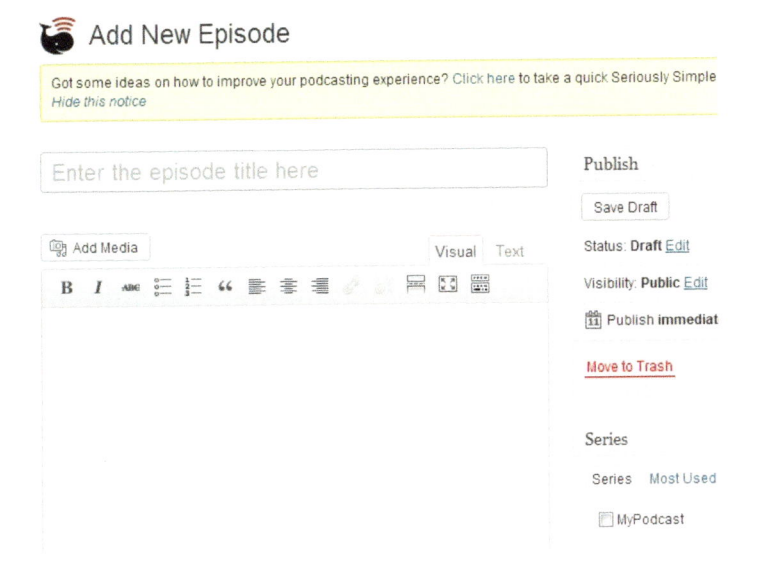

Enter your Title in the uppermost box, and then the Podcast Episode description in the larger editing box below.

Once you've written your post, it's time to upload the audio file itself.

Uploading Your Audio File

On The Podcast Host the process is very simple. Look below the Description box to find the 'Episode Details'. To upload the audio file, click 'Upload File', as shown.

Next, you'll be asked to find your audio file. Click the Select Files button in the middle, as shown below, and find the file on your computer. It will now upload the file to the Podcasting site.

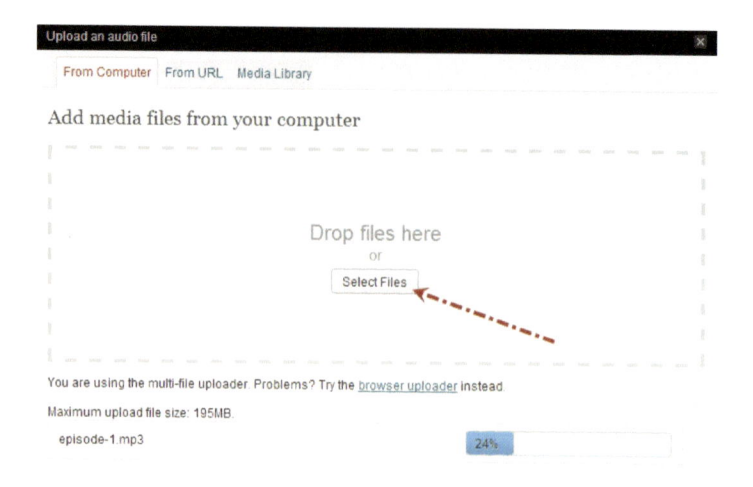

Once the episode is uploaded, enter a descriptive title, and a short description, just for your own reference. Then click **'Insert into Post'**, as shown.

You'll now see the Podcast Episode details shown in the **'Episode Details'** box, such as URL, time and size.

Now, that's all you need to do. The audio file is attached to the episode and ready to go.

Once you've checked everything over, click **'Publish'** to finish the process.

You now have a live podcast!

You can view the episode page now by

clicking the 'View Podcast' link at the top of the page, above the title.

You'll find that a player link has been automatically added so that people can play your episode right from the page, as shown below.

> But, it's not quite over yet. I asked if there was anything more you wanted to cover, and Video Podcasting received a strong vote. So, today I've recorded a Podcast about just that. Have a listen to find out more about the subject:
>
> ▶ ☐ 00:00 / 00:00 ◀ —■
>
> Podcast: Play in new window | Download
>
> And to the task for the day – a nice and simple discussion to round off the fortnight.

They can also download it, or subscribe to it in iTunes – all the things we talked about in the 'Listening to Podcasts' section earlier in the book.

Now all that's left to do is to let people know and get them listening!

Getting Your Podcast Listed

The last step on your podcasting journey is optional, but rare is the person that misses it out. And that's getting yourself listed in iTunes and other directories.

Theoretically your Podcast can now be found and subscribed to. But, it's unlikely anyone will find you without a being listed in the standard directories.

Also, being listed in iTunes makes it very easy for people to subscribe to your Podcast. They can simply find you in the iTunes store, click the subscribe button, and they're done.

Without being listed, listeners have to find your Podcast feed URL and enter it manually into their podcatcher software.

So, let's get listed. I'll go through the process it takes to get into iTunes, and then list some other services you might want to look at.

Registering with iTunes

Unsurprisingly, the first step is to download the iTunes application, if you haven't already. You need to register your Podcast through the iTunes store, and to access that you need iTunes.

Load up iTunes, and click the **'iTunes Store'** button on the top right, as shown below.

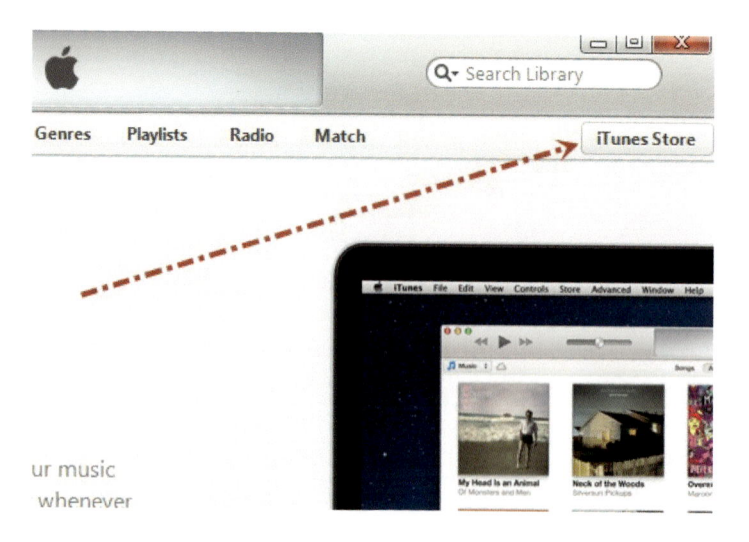

Then, find the Podcast section of the iTunes store by clicking the **'Podcasts'** link at the top of the page as shown in the next screenshot.

You'll see here how many different Podcasts

there are out there, and the variety of topics.

Soon yours will be one of them!

Next, look at the right hand menu and scroll down until you see 'Submit a Podcast'. It'll be in the **Podcast Quick Links** section.

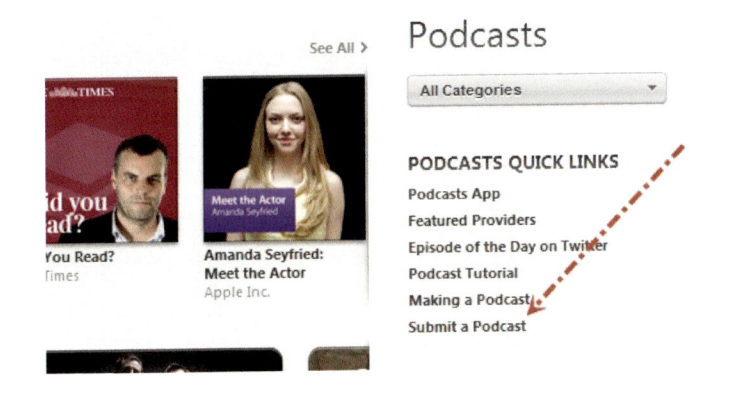

Click 'Submit a Podcast' and you'll be asked to enter the feed URL of your Podcast.

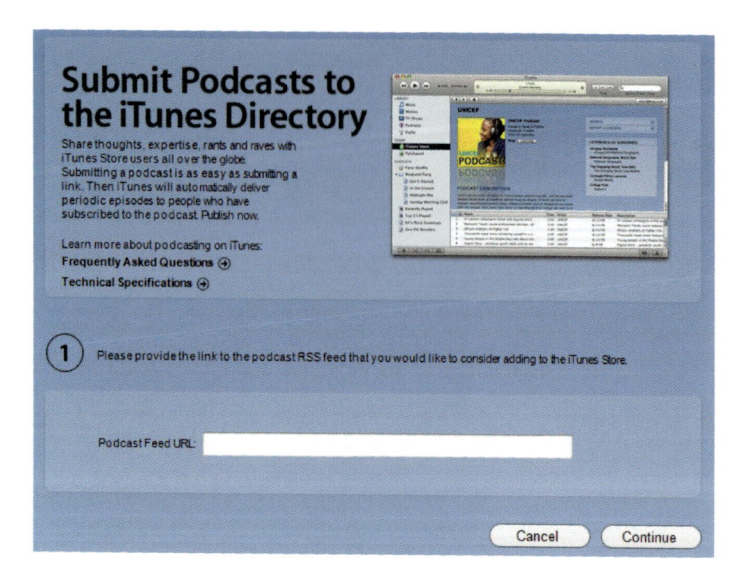

You can find your Feed URL on The Podcast Host by logging into your Dashboard, clicking the Podcast link on the left, and then settings, as shown.

This takes you to your Podcast settings page.

Now, if you scroll to the bottom of the settings page, you'll see a section called 'Share'. In here you'll find your Podcast Feed URL.

Share

Use these URLs to share and publish your podcast feed. These URLs will work with any podcasting service (including iTunes).

| Complete feed: | http://www.thepodcasthost.com/tutorialpodcast/?feed=podcast |
| Feed for a specific series: | http://www.thepodcasthost.com/tutorialpodcast/?feed=podcast&podcast_series=series-slug |

Save Settings

Copy the web address shown next to 'Complete Feed' and paste this into the Podcast Feed URL field currently showing in iTunes.

If you're not already logged in, iTunes will ask you to log in with your Apple ID. If you don't have an Apple ID, you'll have to register with Apple to get one before you can submit your Podcast.

Once you've logged in, you'll see the Podcast detail page in iTunes. This lets you check everything's ok with your submission. If you've already uploaded an image for your

Podcast (found in the settings page, the same one as your feed URL) then that image will appear. The other details can also all be edited on that page, so if anything's amiss click cancel just now. Then you can go back and change the settings before resubmitting your Feed URL.

Once you're happy, click Submit, and you're done! Your Podcast will now be moderated and added to the iTunes store. It might take a few days for this to go through but they should send you an email once it's complete.

Other Podcast Listing Services

There are a few other services worth submitting to once you've released your Podcast.

The first I'll mention is Stitcher. This is a very popular app that appears on both iOS and Android. It lets people find your podcast very easily, and quickly download and listen to it. For that reason, it's worth getting yourself registered.

Next, there are a few directories worth submitting your details to. They are as follows:

- **The Podcast Directory** – Not very imaginatively named, but very big nonetheless.
  URL: www.podcastdirectory.com

- **Podcast Alley** – An institution that's been around since the early days of podcasting. Well worth telling.
  URL: www.podcastalley.com

- **Podfeed.net** – Another large directory that should get you infront of yet more listeners.
  URL: www.podfeed.net

Niche Directories

The last thing I'll mention are niche directories. It's well worth having a look around to see if there are any podcast directories that specialize in your area.

So, if you do a knitting podcast, search in Google to see if there is a knitting podcast directory, or perhaps a craft podcast directory.

An example is the Learn out Loud directory, which lists only Podcasts that teach. To be fair, it's arguable that most Podcasts will teach at some point, but they have their own criteria.

These specialist directories are great because they have much lower competition, and they're much more targeted at your audience. This means it's more likely you'll be spotted amongst the crowd, and by the right type of people.

It's also likely that you'll start to be spotted

by others podcasting in the same niche and so might get a little free promotion when they mention you.

There's nothing like a bit of community for gaining listeners.

Conclusion

That's all folks!

I hope this guide has given you a good introduction to the world of podcasting. I've provided you with enough information to create your very first podcast, and go beyond the simplest form by editing and introducing music.

If you have any further queries about podcasting you can contact me at:

http://www.thepodcasthost.com/contact-us

I'd love to hear what you come up with in future so do send over a link to any podcasts you create - I'd be happy to feedback on them and offer advice.

Good luck with your podcasting efforts, and I'm sure I'll *hear* you out there!

Bonus Chapter

This book is squarely aimed at Podcasting beginners, but I just had to include this chapter for those that are looking to take their podcasting to the next level.

There's one question that's asked more than any other in the Podcasting world...

What's the Best Podcasting Microphone?

I went into this in a little detail earlier in the book, but the microphones shown there are definitely for the entry level Podcaster. Don't get me wrong, you can create great Podcasts with those Mics, and many will happily spend years Podcasting with them.

But, there are always those that like the gadgets and getting hold of the best kit available. For those people, I include this list of the best Podcasting microphones out there.

Before the list itself though, we need to look a little deeper into the categories of microphone. This should arm you with the info needed to decide what's best for you.

Do I Need a Condenser Microphone for Podcasting?

If you want that extra level of depth to your Podcast, it might be worth going for a condenser microphone.

Condenser microphones work in an entirely different, unphathomable way from standard Dynamic mics. But, suffice to say, they introduce a far higher level of quality to your recordings.

The only problem is, because of their sensitivity, they tend to pick up a lot of background noise, so you need a nice quiet recording environment to take advantage of the quality they offer. They also tend to be a lot more fragile, so they're no good for carrying around in your bag.

The other disadvantage is that condenser microphones need external power. This normally comes through a phantom power supply, provided by either a mixing desk, your digital recorder or a battery in the microphone.

Digital recorders or mixing desks are good investments themselves as they provide a lot more flexibility, but that's an extra investment too, and, to be honest, for most Podcasting setups they tend to be overkill.

Essentially, if you want the best quality, but plan to only record from your desk, using a mic stand, in a very quiet environment, then a condenser might be for you.

A good example of an entry level condenser microphone is the Samson C01 Studio Condenser Mic.

High Quality Podcasting Microphones

A little proviso first. When I say high quality, I'm not going to go into the realms of professional mics (such as the Podcaster's dream, the Heil PR40 - http://bit.ly/htp-heil).

I'll look just at those that are within the normal Podcaster's budget, but provide great quality recordings.

These are well above the price range of the mics that I mentioned in the earlier microphones section, but still a fair bit off the £300 or so level of the Heil PR40.

The first in this group are a pair of USB microphones that have been used by Podcasters and general audio producers the world over. The first is the Blue Yeti USB Microphone (http://bit.ly/htp-by) which comes in at around £125.

The Blue Yeti offers amazing quality audio and is amazingly easy to use thanks to it's USB connection. This also by-passes the sound card on your computer, making sure that you get the best quality recording, no matter what equipment your computer sports.

The next, if the Blue Yeti is a little above your budget, is it's little brother, the Blue Snowball Microphone (http://bit.ly/htp-bs). It's RRP is around £85 but I've often seen it on sale at a little over £50. If you can find the snowball at that price, it's an absolute bargain, as it's well worth the RRP price tag.

At this level you can also get some really good quality condenser microphones. I personally use the MXL 990 Condenser Microphone (http://bit.ly/htp-mxl) for all my recording, and mount it on the JamStands JS-MCTB50 Short Mic Stand (http://bit.ly/htp-stand).

I'm not sure what the RRP is, but I found it for £79 and it's been worth every penny. The mic sits on it's stand next to my desk and I pull it up onto the desk every time I need to do a recording.

Conclusion

The two factors that determine what microphone you should go for are:

1. Your recording environment

2. Your Budget.

Buy as expensive a mic as you can afford. As with everything, the more you spend, the better the quality you'll get. But, this only goes up to a point. You can spend hundreds, but you need a lot of knowledge and more professional support equipment to take advantage of the quality offered by the Heil PR40 (http://bit.ly/htp-heil). Save that for a couple of years down the line when you've become an audio production guru, and stick with something like the Blue Yeti for now.

The question of dynamic vs condenser microphone comes down to where you normally record and how much kit you want to use. If you have a nice, quiet regular recording room, then a condenser microphone could be worth buying.

You wont be able to take it anywhere easily, and you will need that mixer or digital recorder to provide the power, unless you find a battery powered mic. But the depth of your recordings will be great, and you'll definitely stand out.

Whatever you choose, enjoy it, and remember that the main thing is, keep on releasing those Podcasts!

Image Credits

The following are creative commons images used in the production of this book:

What Form does a Podcast Normally Take? – Friends Chatting
Paul Downey
http://www.flickr.com/photos/psd/

Mobile Phone Podcast Recording – Smartphones
Phil Roeder – Flickr
http://www.flickr.com/photos/tabor-roeder/

Podcasting Software – Garageband
Trekkyandy – Flickr
http://www.flickr.com/photos/trekkyandy/

Recording Your Podcast – Rockstar
siamesepuppy – Flickr
http://www.flickr.com/photos/siamesepuppy/

Your Recording Environment – Interview
Lee Jordan – Flickr

http://www.flickr.com/photos/leejordan/

To script or not to script? – Reading Brad Flickinger – Flickr
http://www.flickr.com/photos/56155476@N08/

Editing Your Podcast - Mac and Blue Yeti Teaching and Learning with Technology – Flickr
http://www.flickr.com/photos/psutlt/

Music and Sound Effects – Guitar Steve Hardy
http://www.flickr.com/photos/rockmixer/